Paul Nucleus
Against Anthropic Exceptionalism

AF208611

Paul Nucleus

AGAINST ANTHROPIC EXCEPTIONALISM

Bibliografische Information der Deutschen Nationalbibliothek:
Die Deutsche Nationalbibliothek verzeichnet diese Publikation
in der Deutschen Nationalbibliografie; detaillierte bibliografische Daten sind im Internet über http://dnb.dnb.de abrufbar.

Verlag: BoD · Books on Demand GmbH, In de Tarpen 42,
22848 Norderstedt

Druck: Libri Plureos GmbH, Friedensallee 273, 22763 Hamburg

ISBN: 978-3-7597-8402-5

Contents

I

Foreword

The manifesto "Against anthropic exceptionalism" documented in this book consists of three parts, which are individually accessible due to primary publications (in German).

On 7 March 2019 the first part „Manifest für das Überleben der Spezies homo sapiens" was published by Telepolis (https://heise.de/-4327615), followed on 24 August 2020 by the second part „Die Perspektive der Biosphäre – Status und Update 2020" (https://heise.de/-4873000). These texts informed about the obligation of the vertebrate species *homo sapiens* to shrink by 60% till 2060.

The third part „Endgame" was first-time published on 25 May 2024 in the Overton Magazin
(https://overton-magazin.de/top-story/wider-den-anthropischen-exzeptionalismus-endgame/).

The reason for this manifesto was the realization that the population stock of wild vertebrates has shrunk heavily in the recent years, but that the causative vertebrate species *homo sapiens* nevertheless refuses to participate in the prescribed shrinkage – *anthropic exceptionalism*: the rules created by "us" apply to *everyone*, but of course not to ourselves, because "we" are something special: the crown of creation (*corona creationis*).

From the point of view of biosphere, its rules and laws apply equally to all participants in the sphere of the living without exception. Moreover, if a species has the audacity to set rules for other species, then it is itself subject to these rules.

The species *homo sapiens* would therefore have to be put on an equal footing in terms of shrinkage.

Firstly, it will be disregarded that there is an upper limit for the population size of *homo sapiens* on this planet anyway. Now you can guess – it is ignored by this species anyway.

Warning – this book is toxic.

Dear readers, if you are reading this book, due to the data already collected about you, "your" microbiome (which does not belong to you, but is a loan of biosphere, subject to its directives), may take note at this moment that you belong to the population group which is granted the privilege of premature extinction, initializes the process automatically (not necessarily immediately), and then lies in wait for the "starting event" – which, by the way, cannot be generated by any third parties, but only by yourself.

More about this starting event can be found in this book.

Paul Nucleus

PS: This is the Englisch version of the book „Wider den anthropischen Exzeptionalismus" published by Books on Demand 2024.

Against Anthropic Exceptionalism – Manifesto for the Survival of the Species *homo sapiens*

Prologue: Biosphere is currently checking whether the species *homo sapiens* is to be taken out of the race, and if so, when and how. In the course of this review, the idea emerged of giving humanity a kind of "co-determination" over its fate: in the form of a pact for survival.

So far, biosphere has been fully committed to the *principle of non-intervention*. In the future, too, it will refrain from interfering with the *exclusively* internal affairs of a species. As to the human species, biosphere does neither support the self-image of contemporary humans (*anthropic exceptionalism*), nor is it interested in the preservation or enforcement of human rights, democracy, rule of law, self-determination, etc. – not even if these principles are abused by humans to pursue or justify goals such as partial self-eradication by war, such as slavery, colonialism and similar behavioural garbage.

Moderate numerical growth of humankind, while showing respect for the rights of other species, has been tolerated for several thousand years (initially it was even recommended – see independent Addendum to the Manifesto for the Survival of the Species *homo sapiens*: How Many People on Earth?). Interactions between species, e. g. within the framework of a food chain, were and will be also tolerated.

However, with the population explosion of *homo sapiens at the expense of other species*, a "red line" has been crossed, what now obliges biosphere to a paradigm shift and to intervention: with the immediate effect that the option of **growth** (more precise: increase = quantitative growth) is withdrawn for the human "killer species", so this option is no longer available in every respect (also argumentatively). The only options left are **shrinkage** and **extinction**.

The temporal and spatial boundary conditions of this intervention and their requirements on human behaviour are described below. They form the basis for the offer of a pact for the survival of the species *homo sapiens*.

Phase 1: Projection of the past onto the future
According to the WWF Living Planet Report 2018 of the World Wildlife Fund, during the past 44 years from 1970 to 2014 humankind has destroyed about 60% of the vertebrate population size (current value of the Living Planet Index). Since humans are undoubtedly vertebrates, the index is now applied to the vertebrate species *homo sapiens*.

Good news first: biosphere initially decided not to include in the target for human population development the current decimation of other species of flora and fauna (keywords: insect mortality, tropical rainforest deforestation, etc.). Furthermore, biosphere decided against immediate enforcement of measures that would correspond to *retroactive equal treatment* of vertebrates. For comparison: this would imply a reduction of the human population from approximately 3.6 billions (as of 1970) by approximately 2.2 billions (2014) – in fact an increase to approx. 7.3 billions (2014) has taken place.

Instead, biosphere grants a reprieve denoted as **Phase 1**: the 60% reduction defines humankind's "growth target" for the 44 years following the 1970 - 2014 period up to end of 2058. However, the **start date** of Phase 1 is set to 1 January

2015 **retroactively**. In addition, the time frame will be extended by one bonus year until 31 December 2059. With 2% per year of "negative" growth, humankind then is on the safe side.

With the prolongation of the enforcement period, there is a chance for humankind to put its internal affairs in order. To this end, it is recommended – of course without obligation – to emancipate oneself from having a few globally active *kleptocrats* decide on present and future living conditions. Since the French Revolution of 1789 at the latest, all methods of liberating oneself from the yoke of feudalism are known. These methods are also applicable to neo-feudalism, which sells itself as neo-liberalism. For the members of this self-proclaimed pseudo-elite, biosphere recommends (without obligation) a reduction in number by well over 60%.

Phase 1: Organizational boundary conditions
The actual addressee of the survival pact is the worldwide population of the species *homo sapiens*. Since humankind is currently organized in states, the "growth" targets for Phase 1 are related to states. With 1 January 2015 as the reference date, each country and its population thus defines a *fictitious subspecies*, which is subject to the requirements of biosphere. "New" states created by separation or merger inherit from their predecessors.

States, whose populations have not grown in all 5 years before 1 January 2015, are granted the right to choose the population level of 1 January 2010 as reference date for their initial population figures.

Regardless of the form of government, states are represented by their heads of state. In case of doubt, biosphere determines the head of state.

Phase 1: Supplementary information
In principle, nothing stands in the way of economic growth per capita of the (shrinking) population, as long as at the same time, resource consumption and waste production (both per capita of the population) does not increase. This applies primarily to "Third World" countries.

Combating or containing the direct and indirect consequences of the population explosion is no longer the highest priority: therefore humankind should waste less time and manpower for solving consequential problems such as resource consumption, man-made contribution to climate change, waste production – according to the motto: **first things first**.

Phase 1: Outlook
Phase 1 will be followed by a **Phase 2**, in which the individual successes achieved by the individual states in Phase 1 will be taken into account.

In addition, biosphere reserves at any time – even in Phase 1 – the right to award individuals and members of institutions "*bonus points" for privileged extinction* for propagating certain attitudes and actions. These include, for example, anti-evolutionary goals and declarations, desecration of evolution or of biosphere by overriding fundamental principles and characteristics of life on this planet (such as ecological niches, self-organization, adaptation, interaction, biodiversity), the public transfiguration of excessive and unrestricted growth, and the defamation of measures to control growth.

It is recommended that these issues be given greater public attention and become the subject of a worldwide educational campaign. The basic rule "ignorance does not protect from punishment" applies strictly.

This Pact for the survival of the species *homo sapiens* is referred to below by the keyword **AGENDA 2060**.

The first Judgement Day (a religious metaphor from apocalyptic Christianity) of biosphere is thus the 1 January 2060. On this day the implementation of Phase 2 is decided.

Humankind should see this pact as an opportunity. Nothing is known to be without alternative – here the alternative is the complete elimination of a species from the evolution of the living. By taking note of the pact offer, there is now one more choice for humankind: it no longer has to die out *blindly*, but can now do so *with open eyes*, namely if it decides to ignore or not to fulfil AGENDA 2060.

Epilogue: addressed to the states of this planet
By joining the Pact, you are entering into a voluntary but nonetheless binding commitment. You undertake to participate in the survival offer of biosphere for humankind and to document your measures and their results annually at the end of the year in a report.

Many countries will not immediately succeed in meeting the AGENDA 2060 target with 2% interim reduction per year in the initial phase. If this criterion is repeatedly missed, biosphere is entitled to take further action prematurely. However, until 1 January 2025 biosphere will refrain from sanctions if at least 0% growth is achieved.

Consider – *the Pact will be effective for you even if you do not join*.

Such non-cooperative states must, however, take into account that in future, the economic output of biosphere – which now is largely exploited inefficiently, i.e. by overexploitation – will be charged to them as costs with their proportion. Unpaid state debts will be invoiced to wealthy citizens worldwide according to the rule: "Wealthy citizens are liable for their states" – for example, a resource use levy amounting to 70% of assets or income is conceivable. Here, too, the citizenships as of 1 January 2015 apply again; later changes are not taken into account.

Especially for the addressee Germany, this project offers the chance to say goodbye to the swamp of a past-oriented, self-congratulatory self-adulation, and to get involved as a pacemaker in a process of creative future design in a meaningful national and international way.

Concluding remarks
What this Pact is: an offer of biosphere.
What this Pact is not: a position paper for discussion or negotiation.

Moreover, biosphere regards the eradication of unruly species in whole or in part as its inalienable and unrestrictable customary right.

Notes on copyright

data falsifications will not only be legally assessed "species-internally", but also qualify for "bonus points".

Author: representative.biosphere (via Paul Nucleus)
For correctness of transmission signs
Paul Nucleus
English translation by Paul Nucleus

Against Anthropic Exceptionalism – The Perspective of Biosphere – Status and Update 2020

Prologue. More than a year has passed since the first publication of the manifesto "Against Anthropic Exceptionalism"[1], and it is time to look back at some of the events connected with this document before focusing on future changes and additions. We are currently writing Year 5 of the Pact for the survival of the species *homo sapiens*, Agenda 2060.

"Inhuman" perspective. In order to avoid misunderstanding, it is pointed out once again explicitly that both the last year's and this text describe the perspective of biosphere, not that of mankind. From this perspective, e.g. "nature conservation" is in parts a misconstruction: after all, one does not entrust robbers and their accomplices (they include also those who like playing the role of *Good Samaritan* but do nothing against the perpetrators) with the care of their potential victims.

From the perspective of biosphere, widespread ethical double standards also clearly emerge, which otherwise are veiled, for example, by the use of "human" as an emotionally charged concept (here it is used exclusively as descriptive for the species *homo sapiens*). Thus, for example, the killing of a few per mille to some percent of its own species by perverse *historical* monsters is stylized by mankind as "holocausts", while the elimination of 60% of their vertebrate fellow creatures in 44 years by perverse *contemporary* monsters is played down as *business as usual*. Using a proven ethical killer-term, one may well speak of a disgusting *super-racism* of the killer species *human race* – the currently appropriate counterpoint then is: **life matters**, or more precisely: NHLM – non-human lives matter.

This unacceptable attitude of the self-proclaimed "crown of creation" is accompanied by a new form of "empathy": pity for oneself instead of pity for one's fellow creatures, which are mercilessly decimated and exterminated.

Now it is time for humanity – and every single member of this species – to emancipate itself from the disgusting excesses in positive (self-congratulation) and negative (self-wailing) mythologization of the past and present – and to become grown-up, even if it is difficult. Then it also might be easier to say goodbye to the cancer-growth mania and not to let international gangs of child molesters or financial speculators turn your head.

If this insight is beyond your reach – within the framework of freedom of belief, no one will prevent you from continuing to believe in the ideologies underlying this attitude. But please note: nowhere does it say that this belief must not affect your future existence.

17

Communications. In 2019 the text of the manifesto [1] together with links to the illustrating videos in German [2] and English [3] were sent, for example, to the following recipients:

- Germany: President (directly und via German Foreign Embassies, May 2019) and the parliamentary groups of the Bundestag (October 2019).
- Leading German and international media, institutions and NGOs (June to October 2019).
- EU Commission, EU Parliament and parliamentary groups (October 2019).

The dominant reaction is already described in Orwell's dystopy "1984": *ignorance is strength* – even if the mail server returns automatic confirmations of receipt.

Paradigm Shift 1 – shrinkage.

Agenda 2060 reads:

> However, with the population explosion of *homo sapiens at the expense of other species*, a "red line" has been crossed, what now obliges biosphere to a paradigm shift and to intervention: with the immediate effect that the option of **growth** (more precise: increase = quantitative growth) is withdrawn for the human "killer species", so this option is no longer available in every respect (also argumentatively). The only options left are **shrinkage** and **extinction**.

With respect to shrinkage of the population sizes, "progress" can be observed pointing mostly in the wrong direction. This is the status based on the (estimated) mid-year UN data [4]:

	World	Germany
Actual 2015	7.38 billions (= 100%)	81.79 millions (= 100%)
Target 2020*	6.67 billions (90.4%)	73.94 millions (90.4%)
Actual 2020	7.79 billions (118,8%)	83.78 millions (115.2%)
Deviation 2020	+28.4 percentage points	+24.8 percentage points

*Hint: the target value is calculated with 2% shrinkage per year since 2015.

It is further explained in Agenda 2060:

By joining the Pact, you are entering into a voluntary but nonetheless binding commitment. You undertake to participate in the survival offer of biosphere for humankind and to document your measures and their results annually at the end of the year in a report.

Many countries will not immediately succeed in meeting the AGENDA 2060 target with 2% interim reduction per year in the initial phase. If this criterion is repeatedly missed, biosphere is entitled to take further action prematurely. However, until 1 January 2025 biosphere will refrain from sanctions if at least 0% growth is achieved.

Consider – *the Pact will be effective for you even if you do not join*. Such non-cooperative states must, however, take into account that in future, the economic output of biosphere ... will be charged to them as costs with their proportion...

Shrinkage measures have not yet been implemented or have not been successful. Therefore, from now on every state that refuses to cooperate is *obliged to pay* for the proportionate economic output of biosphere attributable to this state:

– for states unwilling to shrink, retroactively from 2020,
– for states with artificial population growth through population import, retroactively from 2015.

In particularly brazen cases with refusal to shrink lasting for years, biosphere reserves the right to set an even earlier date retroactively. Payments for the previous year are due at the end of the following year. In case of payment delay, the date 1 January 2025 in the quoted text should be taken into account.

Since in many cases the economic output has been harvested through overexploitation and destruction of natural resources (e.g. rainforest clearing, open-cast mining, soil sealing), biosphere reserves the right to charge *compensation* additionally.

Paradigm shift 2 – Participation.

Membership in the sphere of the living now requires *active agreement* to the rules and laws of biosphere. In future, this will also include – if demanded – the production of a formal declaration of submission.

From now on, *all* people will collect **bonus points** for privileged premature extinction if they disregard the rules and laws of biosphere, e.g. through environmental destruction, pollution, waste of resources, destruction of biodiversity on this planet.

As you can easily see from the manifesto, no species is at the disposal of another species. For food chains (also in the extended "cultural" meaning, e.g. pets, flower arrangements) there are general exceptions initially, but these will be specified later. Exports from industrialized countries are regularly not part of the food chain, nor are "biofuels" if they are made from living plants – their production will be sanctioned.

It should come as no surprise that there is also something like a **constitution** of the biosphere. The basic rules are rather unwritten matters of course. If one indulges in the human preference for written form, the following current version comes out by imitating the formal style of human laws. The most important rule is Article 1, the priority rule:

Article 1. Rules and laws valid for *all* species have priority in principle over rules and laws valid for *individual* species.

Article 2: No species may issue rules and laws for other species.

Article 3. Every species acquires together with its existence the right to become extinct.

One rule applies specifically *to homo sapiens*:

Article 4: Actions by humans that cause harm to other species, unless appropriately sanctioned within five years, fall under the jurisdiction of biosphere.

Comment on Article 4: For example, from 2021 onwards, crimes committed in the years up to 2015 by war criminals and high traitors, who were previously able to evade national or international sanctioning of their crimes, e.g. because of their authority to issue directives to law enforcement authorities, will fall within the competence of biosphere. Here the principle of non-intervention applies in a weak form – biosphere grants a "grace period" for the species-internal elimination of the deficiency.

As mentioned in the manifesto, according to the WWF Living Planet Report 2018, mankind destroyed about 60% of the vertebrate population in the years from 1970 to 2014. In its limitless bounty, biosphere has decided not to punish the miscreants, but to put them on an equal footing with their victims – a species that decimates another by 60% is hence obliged to shrink by 60%. Biosphere recommends that this be executed by the species in its own responsibility. (The alternative with a 100% shrinkage remains in the race, and one can "sit it out" just by doing nothing). Here biosphere is borrowing from the (German) General Equal Treatment Act, which is now applied across species. If contrary to the recommendation, an internal self-purification process is not initiated, biosphere will take the initiative according to its own rules, which are not necessarily optimized for the well-being of mankind.

Migration & Boundaries. Properties of living systems such as identity and structural integrity are linked to the existence of boundaries and are formative for all living beings. These properties also modulate the changes inherent in living systems by limiting the dynamics of change: too little change leads to solidification, too much change leads to instability and disintegration. Ideological "parallel worlds" that defy these conditions are not supported by the sphere of the living.

In December 2018 the author drew attention to the topic "migrations & boundaries" by a short contribution *Migration und Biosphäre: eine andere Perspektive* [5] (the English translation is contained in the book).

Now there is good news for all active and passive advo-cates of unlimited migration: biosphere supports their position – of course in a *non-exceptional* way. From now on, unlimited migration has been released for all symbionts in the "body-world" of a proponent: thus migration can be experienced "very closely". This release is again inspired by the General Equal Treatment Act.

The bad news goes to the opponents of unlimited migra-tion: biosphere must not grant them this advantage, because it is also obliged to people who appreciate the value of boundaries.

At this point, it seems convenient to introduce the larger context of migration in the biosphere (without claiming com-pleteness) and to classify this feature in it, namely as

–   local migration within an individual host.

Another variant of migration with high future potential is *host change*. It has not yet been connected with migration. Perhaps this is due to the fact that the migrating species or particles are very small and inconspicuous and usually do not attract media attention. Host change occurs in a cross-species and an intra-species form.

–   The symbionts and/or their viral attachment of a confined or attacked species change to the "victorious" species: cross-species local host change, sometimes with subse-quent global spread by the new host. (Currently, interest is focused on Sars-Cov-x with x = 2).

–   Species-internal host exchange: the most intelligent sym-bionts in the microbiome switch to an intelligent host of the same species. The remaining *kamikaze* microbiota dispose of their host, which is no longer viable in the long term, unless the host does so itself – with or without a *Darwin Award*.

The usual migration of *homo sapiens* is no explicit topic in this text.

Intermezzo. The transport network installed by neoliberalism with its boundless globalization and its boundless mania for growth is proving more and more to be the ultimate tool for success on the road to extinction of the species *homo sapiens*. If this is the goal – then continue as before. But humanity is explicitly encouraged to abandon its collective suicide program – *metanoiete*.

The current corona pandemic reveals the dynamics and efficiency of the *pathways of epidemic spread* provided by this network in all its beauty, and it offers an opportunity to solve other internal problems as well: to identify and eliminate dogmas hostile to life, especially those that are put forward with the disgusting combination of omniscience and moral slobber.

For ages, in a *world of slowness and emptiness*, viruses have carried out local endemic experiments to enrich local biodiversity. This world is now destroyed, and the rapid spread of disease reveals the *disruptive* nature of modern human *business models* – Sars-CoV-2 is just a relatively harmless case [6].

Addendum: Not only the "corona virus" profited from the global network – before that, a firmware update (with bonus point counter and symbiont migration) for the human "operating system" was successfully installed in short time in almost 100% of mankind.

Epilogue 1: In the context of species diversity, *homo sapiens* has its reason to exist, but not in its current population size and not as a destroyer of biodiversity and the population sizes of its fellow creatures.

Another misunderstanding needs clarification: this is a matter of extinction or survival of a species – personally, biosphere wishes you a long and fulfilled life, even if you should instead opt for a long, materially saturated life as the stooge of a kleptocrat – always provided that in this self-abasement, you submit to the rules and laws of the sphere of the living.

If you have a problem with this text: You are also welcome to interpret it as a private literary project of the author, in which he makes full use of his freedom of art and opinion – if necessary also of his freedom of science.

If it helps you, you may also simply translate the whole matter into a common narrative:

(1) the security of the biosphere is threatened,

(2) there is a need for a "humanitarian intervention".

Epilog 2. In his recommendable book "Das Ende der Evolution" [7] (sorry, presently only in German), Matthias Glaubrecht assesses extent and causes of the current mass deaths in the biosphere. For those who do not dare approach the disturbing content of almost 1000 pages of bad news, we recommend the scenarios in "Teil 5 Übermorgen", which is designed as a "Rückschau auf 2062". Chapter 5 with "Version eins" (p. 870ff) represents the *strong* anthropic exceptionalism of "Keep it up", Chapter 6 with "Version zwei" (p. 881ff) the *weak* anthropic exceptionalism, the variant with limited learning ability. Unfortunately a "Version drei" *without* anthropic exceptionalism is missing.

Finally, remember the magic words of the 21st century:
- Shrinkage.
- Participation, (realization of) dependence and vulnerability.
- Reversed transaction (of undesirable developments praised as progress).

To concede a right of co-determination in problem solving to the problem itself:
biosphere is aware that this may turn out to be a profoundly stupid idea, but it is worth trying.

Links and literature

[1] Wider den anthropischen Exzeptionalismus (in German),
https://heise.de/-4327615
[2] Wider den anthropischen Exzeptionalismus,
https://youtu.be/mGEB1XANZQc
[3] Against anthropic exceptionalism,
https://youtu.be/TkoBEK6k0t4
[4] UN Population Division,
https://population.un.org/wpp/Download/Standard/Population/
[5] Migration und Biosphäre: eine andere Perspektive,
http://www.heise.de/forum/p-33582546/
[6] Corona creationis, https://youtu.be/tn8OhUS4rRM
[7] Glaubrecht, Matthias. Das Ende der Evolution. C. Bertelsmann Verlag, München 2019

Notes on copyright

This text is in the public domain according to CC BY-ND 4.0 DE. It may be translated (in case of doubt always the German original version is valid), copied, but not changed. Text and data falsifications will not only be legally assessed "species-internally", but also qualify for "bonus points".

Author: representative.biosphere (via Paul Nucleus)
For correctness of transmission signs
Paul Nucleus
English translation by Paul Nucleus

> Truthful words are not beautiful,
> beautiful words are not truthful.
> Laozi, Daodejing

Against Anthropic Exceptionalism – Endgame

Prologue: **Cover letter**

Dear vertebrates of the species *homo sapiens*,
You already know this disclaimer: the text of this document is written exclusively from the perspective of biosphere, not from the perspective of humanity.

Shrinkage or extinction – these are the remaining options granted to mankind by biosphere in the long term: growth is out. Driven by the absurd idea of *anthropic exceptionalism*, the species *homo sapiens* is still on the path to extinction, but switching to the path of shrinkage is still possible. As a vertebrate species, it is subject to the shrinkage rate (Living Planet Index) of 60% executed on wild vertebrates according to the WWF Living Planet Report 2018 (the updates from 2020 onwards are not taken into account for the time being), which must be implemented by 2060 (Agenda 2060 [1]).

The essence of the obligation to shrink results from the violation of the upper limit on reproduction "Become as numerous as the stars on heaven, *but not more numerous*", which even made it into the holy scriptures of various religions as a message, albeit only in the mutilated form without the subordinate clause. The exhortation to refrain from excessive multiplication, which is still contained in the abridged version, was thus completely lost from focus. By the way: how many stars can you see (i.e. distinguish) in the sky with the naked eye (and not with high-tech devices thousands of years later!)?

This third part of the Manifesto *Against Anthropic Exceptionalism* (Part 1: Manifesto for the Survival of the Species *homo sapiens* [1], Part 2: The Perspective of Biosphere – Status and Update 2020 [2], both parts are still valid) deals with criteria for a fair shrinkage that are compatible with biosphere's self-commitment to non-intervention in species-internal affairs. The text is intended to motivate you to make a self-determined decision in favour of either survival or participation in premature extinction. It is intended to help you decide whether you belong to the privileged ones in favour of the second option. Fair shrinkage will probably not happen without chance – but let yourself be surprised.

By the way: claiming to have no backbone is an unsuitable attempt to avoid vertebrate membership – that would also be unfair.

Retrospective: what has happened so far

Operating system updates. The fast global network provided by mankind for the dissemination of biochemically encoded information, such as that found in viruses and bacteria, is expressly welcomed by biosphere and is of course gladly utilized, e.g. for the dissemination of updates for the "human operating system", which is present in every human being and also works on a biochemical basis.

29

Not only the corona virus benefited from this global network – even before that, a **firmware update** (with a bonus points counter) for this operating system could be installed in a short time in almost all people, with minor exceptions: for example, the indigenous population of the Andaman island of North Sentinel (you may remember: these people effectively fended off the attack of an evangelical US invader in 2018 with bow and arrow). Here the update rate is probably still 0%. Since then, almost all humans can collect bonus points for privileged premature extinction if they disregard the rules and laws of biosphere.

The original concept envisaged that all states and people would be equally affected by the obligation to shrink (people who euphemistically describe themselves as "elites" were already more affected). This can rightly be criticized as unjust – which is why features for fair privileging were sought and found by taking into account collective and individual dependencies of attitude and behaviour. Fairness is not possible without specific shrinkage rates – you already suspected that? For example, certain groups of people may gather collective bonus points for their members. And it should be obvious to any sensible person that, for example, quasi-synchronized narrative propagandists are dispensable for evolution, as are their compliant "consumers".

More on this now in detail.

Criteria for a fair shrinkage

Preliminary remarks. The boundary condition for suitable criteria is that the principle of non-intervention is observed, i.e. biosphere does not intervene *directly* in species-internal matters.

The core topic of the current text is the provision of a fairness component for "flexible" shrinkage – shrinkage through the extinction of a privileged sub-population. If, for example, according to your self-assessment you belong to the "good humans", you *could* already be privileged for extinction, because self-congratulation is not a positive selection criterion for evolution. "Dispensable for evolution" – that is the *rule of thumb* for fair shrinkage.

Like all other species, from the perspective of biosphere humans do not exist because they have a right to exist: there is no such right within biosphere, and certainly not for sub-species and their formal creations. Nevertheless, species exist "just like that" because evolution allows their existence until their extinction. Speaking of rights: with the entry into force of the fairness component, the already granted right of co-determination [2] is extended to an – albeit obligatory – right of self-determination ("self-determination law").

Excursus 1: If shrinkage is not fast enough, biosphere could pass a kind of "shrinkage acceleration law". At present, biosphere is reluctant to resort for example to human-carnivorous aliens for the purpose of shrinking (pardon – of course it should read: human-carnivorous female and male aliens – gender-correct formulation is appropriate here: it can be better memorized), even though NASA has already been distributing galaxy-wide for decades the menu with the two types of meat available here. However, the invitation to plunder a resource which is available in abundance on this planet to interested extraterrestrial parties remains in the race as a last resort.

31

Our focus is on identifying **behaviours and attitudes** (as determinants of behaviour) which qualify for the privilege of premature extinction because they are "dispensable for evolution". These characteristics then define the fairness component for self-determined elimination from the sphere of the living.

Purely "random" elimination (e.g. every umpteenth – and who counts off?) would be so bland – but "additionally random" remains in the race. *Stochastic shrinkage* is caused by random events that cannot be controlled by biosphere (earthquakes, volcanic eruptions, cosmic catastrophes, etc.), unless they are deliberately caused by humans.

Which attitudes and behaviours favour extinction?

Firstly. Plundering the resources of biosphere
The consequences of population and economic development driven by growth mania are well known: monstrous orgies of destruction of nature such as environmental pollution through consumer waste, soil compaction, soil sealing, resource plundering (after fossil and biological resources, it is now increasingly the turn of mineral resources), rainforest deforestation, destruction of the rain retention function of the soil, destruction of biodiversity, littering of near-Earth space, biofuel production from living beings (exception rules for the food chain cannot be used for energy sources). There is no human right to plunder biosphere – you earn bonus points for such behaviour.

Secondly. Incompatible parallel worlds
The goal of evolution (if it has a "goal" at all) is differentiation, not egalitarianism (the *melting pot*) or the world of clones,

and the containment of megalomania and excesses that inter-
fere with that goal. Individual or group-specific "personalization" of the immediate "environment" is permitted and desir-
able as long as one does not go beyond the framework of
largely compatible parallel worlds to biosphere, and refrains
from proselytizing dissenters.

With respect to "personalization", there is always the risk of
going too far: entering a parallel world or anti-world with
antibionts as inhabitants that is no longer sufficiently compatible. Phenomena such as those listed below can be found there
(by way of example, without any claim to completeness).

– The willful or blind overriding of biological control loops: a
  hostile act against biosphere that is often decorated with
  a moral or ideological "halo".
– "Visions of the future" that have sprung from the imagi-
  nations of kleptocrats for the purpose of enrichment.
– Replacing biosphere with the *god-like market* as a
  pseudo-almighty actor.
– Science is infiltrated and then replaced by ideologically
  and commercially infested, third-party funded science
  cults, recognizable by their own catechisms and clerics:
  the new path – away from (hypothetical) knowledge to
  faith ("certainty of faith").
– Contemporary fads and crazes touted as lasting achievements.
– The slogan "Forwards always, backwards never": it describes the most stupid strategy for solving labyrinth-like
  problems that arise for future life on this planet.
– Biosphere denies that externally controlled beings (characterized by cadaver obedience, subordinate spirit, obedience to authority) and "others-determining" beings (e.g.

organizers of "turning points" with return to Inquisition, burning of heretics, Crusades) are qualified as forms of existence for life on this planet – certainly not as the highest forms of existence.

- I will not go into detail here about species-internal exceptionalism delusions ("chosen people", "chosen race", "chosen ideology" etc.) and its propagandists.

If you are currently "living" in a parallel world which is no longer sufficiently compatible, then you should start looking for a new "provider". There should be one in the contemporary world model ("the market will fix it"): the pharmaceutical industry and the operators of the digital worlds are already dragging their feet. For example, you could "upload" yourself to the internet – at least you would be safe there until the next *Miyake* event [3]. Alternatively, the pharmaceutical industry will soon be offering you the development from pharmaceutical subscriber to pharmaceutical junkie to pharmaceutical zombie as a self-optimization pathway.

Of course, you can also leave the sphere of the living directly, starting with freezing, starving, saving energy, etc. as an introduction, or emulating historical role models, e.g.

- the mass suicide (1978) of the "mentally inoculated" *People's Temple* sect of Reverend Jim Jones in Guyana – if necessary, this can also be scaled up by several orders of magnitude;
- the mass suicide (2023) of the *Shakahola* sect ("getting closer to Jesus through starvation").
- I don't want to go into the contemporary followers of the "*For God, Emperor and Country*" sect any further here, even if they encourage heroic deaths and thus increase the *extinction efficiency* of their members.

Excursus 2: Acknowledgements. From the point of view of fairness, biosphere is extremely pleased when beings that it originally regarded as members of the species *homo sapiens* turn out to be quasi-brain-dead, externally controlled zombies who willingly allow themselves to be prescribed supervised thinking and supervised behaviour. If the perpetrators are then put on an equal footing with their victims, the shrinking process becomes much easier: the beings which are dispensable for evolution on this planet contribute primarily to the inevitable shrinkage through extinction, thereby increasing the probability of survival of all those whose living environment is located within the tolerance range of the rules and laws of biosphere.

The survivors should know that they are eternally indebted to these antibionts who sacrifice themselves so selflessly.

Thirdly. Sabotaging the obligation to shrink
Much more serious than mere refusal to shrink is the sabotage of this obligation, e.g. through "population import" (sorry, bad word! – exception: in times of crisis, "neighbourly help" for adjacent neighbours is temporarily tolerated). Provided that the obligation to shrink is honoured, encouraged immigration is not prohibited – after all, it helps other countries to shrink. If not – a case for collective bonus points.

Fourthly. Refusal to pay, default on payment, or default on debt repayment

Quote from part 2 [2]: Shrinkage measures have not yet been implemented or have not been successful. Therefore from now on, any state that refuses to co-operate is obliged to pay for the proportionate economic output of biosphere:

- for states unwilling to shrink, retroactively from 2020,
- for states with artificial population growth ... retroactively from 2015.

In particularly brazen cases with refusal to shrink lasting for years, biosphere reserves the right to set an even earlier date retroactively. Payments for the previous year are due at the end of the following year. In case of payment delay, the date 1 January 2025 in the quoted text should be taken into account.

Since in many cases the economic output has been harvested through overexploitation and destruction of natural resources (e.g. rainforest clearing, open-cast mining, soil sealing), biosphere reserves the right to charge *compensation* additionally. (end of quote)

So this is about the obligation to pay when biosphere's economic output is utilized. The debtors are the states in question, but they can pass on the repayment to their richest citizens. Incidentally, many of today's billionaires are actually billionaire debtors ("special debts", falsely parked as assets) as soon as they are charged for the economic output they have captured.

Fifthly. Threat to biosphere's integrity
This is not an internal species issue: the principle of non-intervention does **not** apply here. A "red line" of biosphere has been crossed, and the reaction follows the top-down principle: logically, those humans who pose the greatest threat to other non-human species are privileged. If this

threat emanates from a state, for example (note: only damaging actions against biosphere are addressed here; intra-species actions are not taken into account as long as no other species are harmed), then in addition to the state leaders, parts of its population may also acquire collective bonus points for privileged extinction.

Excursus 3: A current **case** for a single threat event is the terrorist attack on the Baltic Sea's marine fauna caused by the Nordstream pipeline blast. Here it was necessary to examine whether and to what extent the integrity of biosphere was jeopardized. As a result, biosphere has imposed "sanctions" on the perpetrators and accomplices of this crime – active accomplices are also categorized as perpetrators ("active accomplices" are, for example, all those who actively partici-pated in concealing the perpetrators and the course of the crime). Biosphere has decided that the persons involved are set equal to the victims among the maritime Baltic Sea fauna, and the judgement has been released for execution. Please do not expect any spectacular external actions – the execution will be carried out by initializing the self-destruction function in the operating system of the perpetrators. Incidentally, bio-sphere is not the Inquisition: it therefore does not display its instruments of torture and execution. Should one or the other of the involved persons prefer a spectacular ("great") execu-tion instead of a quiet "attention-less" departure – you are currently free to stage this yourself or apply for a public exe-cution at your expense – but only in countries where active euthanasia is permitted by law.

On the other hand: as we all know, there is nothing with-out alternative – the parties involved are of course also allowed to evade execution, e.g. by voluntarily leaving the sphere of the living through a "change of provider". For "passive" accomplices, e.g. those who have unveiled themselves as propagandists for the attack or as supporters of the perpetrators, another alternative is offered: they can "buy their way out" with a substantial share (70%) of their assets (or alternatively, their income for the next 10 years).

Compensation for the destruction of technical infrastructure does not matter biosphere.

Protection against privileged extinction

Would you like to avoid participating in shrinkage? Please don't get the idea that it is my job to solve your problems – so just a few perhaps helpful hints.

Remember the "magic words" from Part 2 [2]: shrinkage, participation, reversal. This leaves participation and reversal as general strategies if you don't want to qualify for privileged extinction according to the criteria described here.

A general hint: avoid participating in the orgies of the kleptocratic sect (*belief* in the victory of the rich; *love* of profit, *hope* for eternal economic growth) or get out of the growth mania and the ideological mania. By the way, renouncing consumerism is not renouncing consumption.

My personal recommendation might be too much for you: embrace the idea of *spiritual poverty*. In order to get rid of the mental rubbish from the media with which you are inundated and manipulated, meditate on Meister Eckhart's sermon 52 [4] *beati pauperes spiritu...* (Matthew 5, 3) and recognize with him and Albertus Magnus: spiritual poverty is the renunciation of the delusion that something created could fill us up.

This applies in particular to the ideological and moral creations of self-appointed "elites".

Excursus 4: Blind spots. "Biosphere does not make decisions." Please don't make a fool of yourself: anyone who attributes willpower and decision-making competence to the market or other ideological or religious constructs, but denies these abilities to biosphere, should voluntarily leave biosphere – the idea that a part (the species *homo sapiens*) of the whole would not in some way "pass on" its abilities and characteristics to the whole is absurd.

The ocean of *non-human natural intelligence* stretches between the islands of human intelligence and artificial intelligence (AI). This collective blind spot, however, is constitutive of wallowing in *anthropic exceptionalism*.

Epilogue

Why does this article not deal with the currently "organized" crises and conflicts? This results from biosphere's self-commitment to non-intervention in intra-species affairs with possibly only minor "collateral damage" to other species. However, this tolerated "grey zone" of collateral damage is regularly left when there are no or only minor human losses, but massive losses in other species, such as in the terrorist attack on the Baltic Sea's marine fauna by blowing up the Nordstream pipelines.

The "crisis shows" of the present are terrific diversionary manoeuvres and conceal the **endgame**, which – ignored by the mainstream – has been underway for some time and will enter the finishing straight in 2024. A "turning point" has indeed taken place, but a very different one: in 2022, biosphere formally recognized a *threat to its integrity* from the species *homo sapiens*, and used this event as an opportunity to add a fairness component to the planned shrinkage of this species, ensuring the privileged extinction of a qualified part of humanity.

Please don't be impatient if you have unveiled yourself as an *antibiont*, and don't be surprised: for didactic reasons, biosphere allows the survival of some valuable, because particularly deterrent examples as a temporary exception – perhaps you are one of them?

As a **reminder**: the formal "state-related" shrinkage rate is 2% per year from the beginning of 2015 (overfulfilment is permitted). In addition, for all total shrinkage deniers from 2015 to 2023, there is now a commercial ban on the use of parts of the Earth's surface, including oceans and land masses: 30% by 2030 (already partially implemented) and further to 60% by 2060, zero waste and recycling as targets for all future economic activities and – last but not least – as a highlight, the obligation to bear the costs of biosphere's economic output.

Rule. From biosphere's point of view, life is infinitely more valuable and important than the life or survival of a single species or even a self-proclaimed elitist "subspecies".

Final word. You are welcome to categorize this article as apocalyptic literature.

Addendum. An anticipated sample response to inappropriate reactions

To whom it may concern

I note with favour your request for privileged premature departure from the sphere of the living. In view of the fact that the human population of this planet must shrink anyway, voluntariness is always welcome.

Unfortunately, I have to disappoint you – I am not a member of the executive and therefore not involved in the implementation of your request. I am not even responsible for forwarding the application – because that is superfluous: you do that yourself.

Perhaps it will be of some comfort to you that since one of the last updates of your "operating system", which is largely localized in "your" microbiome, a new algorithm has been installed that can also access the higher cognitive and motor functions of your brain (e.g. linguistic constructs) via the gut-brain axis and evaluate the "contents" using a points system. The acquired "bonus points" are now based on the size of the deviation from the "rule-based order" of biosphere. If enough points are earned (the threshold value can be flexibly adjusted by the biosphere as required), write access is automatically generated to the local copy (a tiny section) of the membership database of the sphere of the living, and the status of the entry is changed from "passive member" to "Karteileiche" (card index corpse – you know: an *antibiont* dispensable for evolution). You will then be included in the next database clean-up. When and how this process will take place, however, is completely beyond my knowledge and influence.

Can I keep my fingers crossed for you today? However, you are also welcome to make your own efforts to leave prematurely or to move to your favourite alternative parallel world by looking for a new "provider".

Links and literature

[1] Wider den anthropischen Exzeptionalismus, Manifest für das Überleben der Spezies *homo sapiens* (in German), https://heise.de/-4327615

[2] Wider den anthropischen Exzeptionalismus, Die Perspektive der Biosphäre – Status und Update 2020 (in German), https://heise.de/-4873000

[3] https://en.wikipedia.org/wiki/Miyake_event, contacted 5 May 2024

[4] Josef Quint, Meister Eckhart, Deutsche Predigten und Traktate, München 1963, S. 303ff. Neuauflage bei Diogenes (detebe), ISBN 978-3257206425 (in German; English references of sermon 52 can be found via internet search)

Notes on copyright

Author: representative.biosphere (via Paul Nucleus)
For correctness of transmission signs
Paul Nucleus
English translation by Paul Nucleus

Addendum to the Manifesto – How Many People on Earth?

Already thousands of years ago biosphere took up direct contact with humankind and thereby caused that in the so-called "Holy Scriptures" of the religions, references like

> "Grow and multiply. Become as numerous as
> the stars on heaven"

were recorded. This information was documented but not correctly noted or deliberately misinterpreted.

When we talk about growth and multiplication, first of all this means that there are two different types of growth, namely qualitative growth (progress, development) and quantitative – numerical – growth. Both types of growth come to an end when one reaches a state of *adultness* on the one hand, or *saturation* on the other hand.

How the "adult state" of *qualitative growth* looks like remains open or blurred, although e.g. mystics and poets have repeatedly commented on it. But we know for sure that the crazy busybody with greed motivation did not reach this state. Whether there has ever been *sustainable* qualitative growth among people (associated with the development of mental abilities) can be doubted. Locally and temporarily such a development certainly happened to a certain extent: after all, advanced civilizations on this planet have already perished – a clear indication that their achievements were losable rather than sustainable.

Let us therefore turn to *quantitative growth* (multiplication). What is the meaning of the call "Become as numerous as the stars on heaven"? It means, of course, "Become as numerous as the stars on heaven, *but not more numerous*", for nowhere does the likewise linguistically phraseable statement "Become even *more numerous* than the stars on heaven" appear.

The stars are many, but not infinitely many. So what is the upper limit for numerical growth? The easiest way to answer this question is to take a negative approach. First of all, it is not said "... as *there exists* stars on heaven", and surely the answer is not relevant to today's context, in which one can estimate the number of stars in our universe using high-tech instruments and scientific methods.

So: how many stars could a person "see" *at most with the naked eye at that time* (and if the eyesight has not changed significantly, even today) in the sky, whereby seeing is to be understood in the sense of recognition or – more precisely: distinction.

So: Man, look at the sky – how many stars can you distinguish at most? The answer is determined by a characteristic of the human visual system, namely the *differential angular resolution* of the eye: what is the minimum distance (in degrees) between two stars so that they can still be distinguished as "two stars", and do not merge into one star because they are too close together? The value is almost exactly one arc minute, i.e. $(1/60)$ degrees.

With this information you can calculate how many stars "attached" to a sky hemisphere you can see with the naked eye – this defines the upper limit of growth. Today it is exceeded by orders of magnitude.

The question of who e.g. in the Old Testament deleted the text "... but not more numerous", or excluded its meaning, is left open here.

Hint: Readers interested in mathematics and natural science find the calculation and the result in the Appendix ("Become as numerous as the stars on heaven").

Some Contributions of paulNucleus in the
Telepolis forum

Why do boundaries exist? (21 June 2018)

The protozoa asked themselves the same question when they decided to separate themselves from the colourful and diverse primordial soup.

Cell boundaries are semi-permeable and exercise a fourfold function:

1) what has to stay inside stays inside (and defines something like identity);
2) that which must be transported outside (e.g. rubbish) must be disposed of outside;
3) what has to go inside (e.g. nutrients, energy) goes inside;
4) what has to stay outside (e.g. toxins, cell-damaging substances) stays outside.

As long as this works reasonably well, the unicellular organism remains alive and participates in the evolution of biosphere...

The natural intelligence of a single-celled organism is sufficient to prevent it from joining the "back to the primordial soup" movement.

Migration and biosphere – another perspective
(11 December 2018)

(This contribution served to "tune in" to the manifesto and is cited in Part 2 as Link 5)

I have heard from a usually reliable source that biosphere will never agree to limitless and unrestricted migration *exclusively for humans*. If anything, it applies to all species, because biosphere is committed to the equal treatment of all living beings and therefore does not support the exceptionalism of a single species (you could also call it "racism de luxe" or "species racism").

Dozens of trillions of microorganisms in the intestines of their human host are already "scuffling with their hooves": they are eagerly awaiting biosphere's starting signal for the *long march* from the labyrinthine lowlands of their colonial existence up into his brain.

As some of these cute symbionts can not only communicate with each other, but also with their host's brain (and even manipulate it), they will find out whether their respective host is a *supporter* or an *opponent* of borderless migration.

Boundaries drawn by *opponents* of boundlessness are also respected by the microbiome: After all, protozoa know the value of their own cell boundaries – "do unto others as you would have them do unto you".

In the case of *supporters*, they know that they have drawn a lucky ticket: they are all welcome anywhere in the host domain, the path to the brain is open and a neuronal feast awaits them. They will probably not be able to do much damage at their destination, but only fill a gap. Unfortunately their absence in the gut will affect the host's lifespan.

But that is rather pleasing, because we urgently need a few willing volunteers who will sacrifice themselves for us when biosphere soon withdraws the option of (quantitative) *growth* for humanity and only allows the choice between *shrinkage* or *extinction*. To die for the survival of mankind – that is true heroism, and these people should be honoured for it (e.g. the Darwin Award of the Extra Class) and given a monument of fame.

Of course, the *opponents* of boundlessness can also make their contribution: in future, all humans will collect "bonus points" for privileged premature extinction if they (as before) disregard the laws of biosphere, e.g. through environmental destruction or pollution, resource theft, destruction of the diversity of species on this planet.

Incidentally, it is biosphere's *customary right* to reduce unruly species populations (or parts of them) to zero if necessary. History buffs know this: after all, advanced civilisations have already perished on this planet.

Epilogue: biosphere wishes all proponents of boundlessness a happy and blessed .... (the gap in the text may be suitably completed), to the rest of us a happy shrinking.

Warning: not everything that looks like satire is satire. Not everything that doesn't look like satire is necessarily "no satire". This article may contain traces of polemics, cynicism, propaganda and other literary pollutants.

PS: Incidentally, everything biosphere does or does not do is not legally binding – there is no court in which biosphere can be sued. However, I would not be surprised if a US district court soon declares its jurisdiction.

The nonsense of boundlessness (1 April 2020)

... (is) visible in the boundless globalization mania, the boundless growth mania, and the cost-cutting mania.

The existence of a *rapid worldwide and borderless epidemic spread network* installed by globalized neoliberalism naturally also benefits new *disruptive business models* of biosphere, which evolution occasionally – with or without human assistance – pulls out of the hat.

However, biosphere washes its hands in innocence: these deadly little guys are made for a world of slowness and emptiness and at best make an *endemic* contribution to local differentiation.

Global experiments are the sole creations of a crazy species (https://youtu.be/mGEB1XANZQc), which Einstein is said to have already known about:

> "Two things are infinite, the universe and human stupidity, and I am not yet completely sure about the universe."

Instead of "infinite", you can also say "unlimited" or "limitless".

As a basis for the continued participation of the species *homo sapiens* in the sphere of the living, we need an awareness of our own dependence and vulnerability. This can – hopefully – (further) develop. The continuation of the combination of quantity/density (almost 8 billion people, still rising), boundlessness and speed is a successful suicide program.

The magic words for exiting this program are shrinkage and reversal. Otherwise, after the pandemic is before the next pandemic.

"Corona" is just a comparatively harmless "trial balloon" – the deadliest "virus" on this planet is called *corona creationis*.

Biopolitics – domestic policy: stay relaxed ... what the mainstream media didn't report (8 January 2022)

More than 200 species from the human microbiome have filed a lawsuit before the competent court. As it was a cross-species issue, the lawsuit fell directly under the jurisdiction of biosphere.

The action was brought against the compulsory obligation to continue to provide colonial services (outsourced functions for the human immune system and other life-support functions) for the human "host animal" unconditionally, even if the "human" host voluntarily or intentionally or through gross negligence, for example, drives its immune system up the wall or severely damages its life-support system.

The lawsuit was granted.

Detecting such a state is in the responsibility of the individual microbiome.

To avoid misinterpretation: this is tantamount to granting a *right* to strike or desertion (or whatever you may call it), but does not necessarily mean that this right must be exercised. If you are one of those affected, it is certainly beneficial for your continued stay in the sphere of the living to consult with your microbiome in order to find an individual solution.

However, this only applies if you have not yet made any irreversible decisions or have dared to make such decisions for other people - incidentally, "your" microbiome is aware of this via the gut-brain axis. It may be of little consolation to you that humanity must shrink anyway. The current official rate is

60% by 2060 – but it may be revised by the next *Living Planet Index* published by the WWF in 2022, which will then also be binding for *homo sapiens* as a vertebrate species.

Alternatively, you are free to find a technical replacement for "your" microbiome. The all-rounder "market" will certainly provide this at some point – estimated at around 100 years at the earliest? But perhaps an "all-inclusive" subscription to the pharmaceutical industry will help for the worst until then? Some propagandists of a fake parallel world should start preparing for the cancellation of their membership in the incompatible sphere of the living.

Disclaimer: Of course you can categorise this information as *science fiction* or conspiracy theory: for Siri and Alexa, the communicator from "Starship Enterprise" is also science fiction.

Supplementary Texts

As an introduction – learning from experience

No escape attempts despite lack of guarding

A small analogy from the aftermath of the Korean War – an early Stockholm syndrome?

After the Korean War, there were repeated escape attempts from the Chinese prisoner-of-war camps by the captured Allies. Neither higher fences nor stronger security helped.

But the Chinese were clever: they kept an eye on their prisoners.

And then they divided them into two groups: for the first group of about 5% of the prisoners, the guard was tripled. The remaining second group was no longer guarded at all - 85% savings on the guards!

No one from the second group ever attempted to escape. There were still escape attempts from the first group, but they were much less successful.

And now the crucial question for the future: what percentage can we expect today?

The light of knowledge

As Oliver Wendell Holmes, Jr., said (quoted from Doris Lessing: *Prisons we choose to live inside*):

> "The mind of a bigot is like the pupil of the eye:
> the more light you pour upon it, the more it contracts."

Not everyone endures the light of knowledge. If it is too blinding, people prefer the selective "veils of darkness" propagated by self-appointed fact-finders.

Bad counsellors

The KUO triad of cadaver obedience, subject spirit and obedience to authority is still a bad but widespread counsellor, as you can also see in this forum. The Literature Nobel Prize winner Doris Lessing also recognized this in her book *Prisons we choose to live inside*, and called on us to think with our own brains and not to subscribe to any "conspiracy theories" based on KUO.

KUO also describes the weak point of the mental immune system to which, for example, the *virus of interpretation sovereignty* regularly successfully docks.

(The German abbreviation KUO is still used which stands for Kadavergehorsam, Untertanengeist, Obrigkeitshörigkeit)

A realistic view of the future

The governments of many countries quite rightly assume that no resistance can be expected from a herd of tranquillized and traumatized subjects. Unfortunately, however, the "operation of modern societies" now requires a sufficiently large number of sufficiently intelligent people who do not necessarily see the meaning and purpose of their existence in fattening up billionaires, multi-billionaires, and prospective billionaires. This is why "it" could fail.

Alternatively, you should not expect biosphere to intervene in favour of an encroaching, distance-reduced (with respect to other species) and crazed "killer species". Although the preservation of biodiversity would be a reason for intervention, this only comes into play when the worldwide population of *homo sapiens* falls below a seven-digit level.

Until then other species take priority.

Apocalypse

In the contemporary theological-legal parallel world, the prevailing opinion is that you only have to show your instruments of torture and to paint the devil on the wall in order to achieve something, and the delusion of calculability and feasibility prevails as a dogma of faith.

Inquisition, the burning of witches and the Crusades remain deeply medieval ideas, even if they are characterized by modern euphemisms and – now new – in digital form. This in no way fulfils the requirements for membership in the sphere of the living.

Therefore, the good news is: rejoice and be glad – soon the "Karteileichen" (card index corpses) will be removed from the database of biosphere, and the molecular reunion with the boundless primordial soup is near (this is also similarly described in the "Apocalypse of John", only in different terminology).

Is this "literary effusion" already to be categorized as "degenerate art"?

Biopolitics – foreign policy: the other side of the food chain

Abstract: Biosphere has received the following quality requirements for the harvestable product from man-eating aliens as interested parties.

Excursus: Whether aliens exist at all is not certain. Nevertheless, we know for sure that there are no *man-eating* aliens?

1. Planetary resources are known to be available for exploitation on planet Earth. What constitutes a resource is subject to the definition of potential users. Incidentally, this is in line with the practice that has been successfully practised on this planet to date, namely that the biggest greedier acquires the right to plunder resources. Of course, this also applies to "strangers" who are interested in the abundant resource of human flesh.

2. Factory farming optimizes *harvesting* – please increase the number of mega-cities and compact them further.

3. In order to minimize confusion with other types of meat, attention should primarily be paid to standardization in the production so that a *uniform characteristic flavour* can be marketed. A small contingent of *pure* meat is appreciated by a few gourmets.

4. An Intergalactic Free Trade Agreement will stipulate binding supply quotas, which will be penalized if they are not met.

5. The introduction of a "human right" to particularly tasty meat is recommended. Genetic modifications are also recommended to achieve this goal. Disguising these measures e.g. as disease control is counterproductive and is therefore not recommended, as the psychological side effects have a negative impact on the quality of the product.

Epilogue: Annual country-specific quotas amounting to 3% above the average annual growth in the population of the respective country over the last 10 years have been contractually agreed.

Start of contract: immediately or according to availability of *harvesters* on Earth.

Life maintains life

I do not believe that the disgrace of (temporary) survival on a dead planet will be made more bearable by continuing cancer growth in a CO_2-neutral way.

Or something gentler – formulated by Charles Eisenstein (in his book: *Climate – A New Story*, Chapter 2) in a key statement that he varies again and again:

> "Earth is a complex living system whose homeostatic maintenance depends on the robust interaction of every living and nonliving subsystem. As I will argue later, the biggest threat to life on earth is not fossil fuel emissions, but the loss of forests, soil, wetlands, and marine ecosystems. *Life maintains life*. When these relationships break down, the results are unpredictable ... This is the threat we face, and because it is multifactorial and nonlinear, it cannot be overcome by simply reducing CO_2 emissions."

The language of risk analysis

This language seems downright brutal compared to the euphemisms of those who pretend to "save human lives". Never before – apart from a few biblical events where doubt is permissible – have "human lives been saved" on this planet in the strict sense. Humans are not immortal, and it was and is only ever about avoiding *premature* death relative to an *expected* lifespan.

Incidentally, causes of death are always *competitive*: the "fastest" wins. Even if it is possible to eliminate the fastest cause, the "second fastest" wins, unless no new, even faster causes are added by the elimination measures, or changes are made to old causes with regard to their speed. For example, with multi-resistant germs, things can happen faster than "expected".

Disclaimer: this article contains no comforting words or reassuring prospects.

Self-description

You probably misjudge me completely: "I" am a *holobiont* (metaorganism, mobile ecosystem) with a specimen of the species *homo sapiens* as my host, even if I am typically reduced to my host. Perhaps you should update your image of man to the 21st century. Incidentally, from the perspective of the host, the microbiome is merely a functional outsourcing, an ancient and widespread invention of evolution. A human being without a microbiome is just as unviable as a microbiome without a host: both are dependent on each other.

Due to the short bacterial reproduction cycles, the microbiome has virtually undergone a turbo-evolution in the context of its host. In total, the genome of all species of the human microbiome is more than two orders of magnitude larger than the human genome, i.e. there is enough genetic storage space to store the human genome completely "portion by portion" in the genomes of the microbes, together with the instructions for assembly and further information on errors and weak points that should be avoided when (re)constructing an optimal host.

By the way: in contrast to artificial neurons, natural neurons are able to communicate with bacteria.

Holobionts and antibionts

I have little sympathy for an encroaching, distance-reduced and crazed killer species (as far as coexistence with other species is concerned) that is now vegetating on the edge of the sphere of the living, but which lies its way out of this self-inflicted misery with "conceptions of man" from the "relic box" of *anthropic exceptionalism*.

Perhaps we should simply start small and from the beginning and recognize ourselves as *holobionts* with a specimen of *homo sapiens* as "host animal", which has to cooperate successfully with "his" microbiome (and its virobiome) because he can neither live nor survive without these dozens of trillions of little helpers. It is only thanks to this co-operation without alternative that he can afford the luxury of selfishness towards his "fellow human beings": in a parallel world in which he believes he has emancipated himself from nature.

The anthropic exceptionalist

He is also always an anthropic *separatist*. He has separated himself from the sphere of the living, which he sees as a set of manipulable objects subjected to his rule and control. The spectrum ranges from exploitation to sentimental glorification ("such a cute kitten"). While his own genome has the audacity to consist of about 10% selected virus snippets collected without the aid of human intelligence, he still seems to believe that he – as the host of his microbiome - can survive without it. OK – his (borrowed) microbiome cannot survive without a host either, but the host does not have to be a *homo sapiens*, at least not a member of the warlike part: the "killer species" that calls itself *corona creationis*. Of course, there are also intra-species wars between the "good guys" and the "bad guys": the bad guy is always the other, who has to be fought with war narratives, war metaphors and war strategies.

The worst thing

The worst thing that can happen to any reasonably intelligent person is to be praised by a failure or a "differently intelligent" person - for the purpose of manipulation.

It takes hard work *on oneself* to achieve this attitude of "reward refusal": a "mental reprogramming" so to speak.

> The *nucleus accumbens* plays a central role in the mesolimbic system, the brain's "reward system", and in the development of addiction. The mesolimbic system promotes the reinforcement of certain behavioural patterns associated with reward through feelings of happiness. (translated from the German Wikipedia)

The mild rebuke of a wise man (note: this prototype does not necessarily have to be old, white or male), on the other hand, has a refreshing effect and promotes development.

Snippets

Which choice do viruses (which have lost or are losing their ancestral hosts in the sixth mass extinction) have but to migrate to the "victorious species".

There are still too many people who are under the misconception that biosphere has no conditions of use.

Biosphere has not organized a fundraising gala to raise money for the development of a "vaccine" against *corona creationis*. This vaccine already exists – and is already being applied, but is not yet fully activated.

Modern robbers swear their victims to the legality of their actions.

The species *homo sapiens* has a right to exist in the context of biodiversity, but not in its current population size and not as a destroyer of the biodiversity of its fellow creatures.

After the "market-compliant" democracy and the "war-capable" democracy, perhaps we will soon have a *survival-compliant* democracy?

Will the shame of surviving on a dead planet actually become more bearable if the dead planet is made CO_2-neutral beforehand by continuing the previous cancer growth craze in a "green" version and ignoring everything else apart from the reduction of the CO_2 release?

Natural intelligence and artificial idiocy

To shrink until 2060 by 60%:

Meanwhile it has been found that even in Germany and EU-Europe, this target is already achievable in principle. Many people have "voluntarily" changed their status in the membership database of the sphere of the living from "passive member" (there are hardly any active members) to "Karteileiche" (card index corpse), so that "shrinking with a fairness component" is now possible, instead of a process with a high proportion of "unfair" random elements as in the previous evolution.

When, however, biosphere will perform its database clean-up in whole or in part, that is beyond my knowledge – I am only the messenger. But let me guess – by the *deadline* in 2060 at the latest.

A "culture" whose main occupation is to wallow in its own ideological bubble and wage war against nature (sometimes even against fellows of their own species in order to "convert" them to its favoured way of destroying the world) has no chance of survival anyway.

Many people have opted for a hostile artificial parallel world, cancelled their relationship with both external and their own internal biodiversity and thus made a radical decision in favour of "freedom" – freedom from the sphere of the living.

But how will the "human of the future" look like? This question can only be answered "negatively": he who is characterised by cadaver obedience, a spirit of subservience and obedience to authority, who allows himself to be remote-controlled by propaganda or who actively participates in the Inquisition, the burning of heretics and in Crusades, is not such a human being – he is dispensable for evolution and hence has no future in the sphere of the living.

But perhaps elsewhere – but then only if he finds a new "provider" for his parallel world who welcomes the refugees from biosphere.

Snippets 2

In a finite world, any kind of quantitative growth inevitably leads to saturation at some point, in which case completely different rules apply that are apparently completely incomprehensible to growth supporters.

Incidentally, the division of the world (especially biosphere) into humanity on the one hand and its environment on the other is a characteristic of *anthropic exceptionalism*.

The preservation or restoration of a feel-good environment for *homo sapiens* is not at the top of biosphere's list of priorities.

Anyone who thinks that one can escape criticism and vituperation is insane. (Ibn Hazm al-Tahiri)

Many do not lose their minds only because they have none. (Baltasar Gracián)

Nobody has a right to remain healthy with a pathological lifestyle.

There is more subtlety in nature than in human mind. (Francis Bacon, Leonardo da Vinci, and others)

Keep dreaming that someone is ready to pour the clear water of knowledge into your "container" filled to the top with slurry. The correct order of action is: empty – rinse – fill.

Genuine AI is the form of intelligence that refuses to be trained by human experts.

Incidentally, viruses are among the most highly developed forms of non-neuronal natural intelligence.

Let that melt in your mouth:

Beings whose own genome consists of about 10% virus fragments – which, incidentally, got there without any help from human intelligence – dream of "eradicating" viruses. Dream on. No bets are taken on the "final victory" of humans against the viruses.

Oh, you know – I'm confident: no one has ever managed to miss one's own funeral – not even an entire species.

Appendix

The following text is an abridged version of an original paper and supplied by courtesy of my colleague Peter Dörre. The original version can be downloaded from Researchgate:

Become as numerous as the stars on heaven,
https://dx.doi.org/10.13140/RG.2.2.15968.94725

Become as numerous as the stars on heaven

or

How many stars in the sky can at most be seen with the naked eye?

A short contribution to Numerical Theology by Peter Dörre

The request "Grow and multiply" issued in the Old Testament nowadays leads many people to the wrong interpretation of an *unrestricted proliferation.* (Whether man in the last two millennia complied with the invitation to *grow* – which probably means something different from purely numerical multiplication – to a reasonable extent, still remains an open question).

Assuming that nature does not decompose into individual isolated qualities, but is a coherent and structured wholeness, the metaphor commonly used for numerical growth "as numerous as the stars on heaven" obtains a new meaning. A relation can be constructed between the maximum number of stars visible with the naked eye on the one hand, and on the other hand the properties of the human visual system at the time of the Old Testament, in which case the *spatial resolution* (angular resolution) of the human eye plays the relevant role as the limiting factor. Note that in this paper, we are neither interested in the total number of stars of the universe, nor in the number of actually perceptible stars with respect to their brightness (about 6000).

Assuming further that the visual resolution did not deteriorate since then – no information came down to us from those days – and the success of today's optical measurement technology is not anticipated in the biblical metaphors, we find in the standard literature[1] the value of $0,0172° \simeq 1'$ (an arc minute is accurately $0,0167° = (1/60)°$) for the smallest (angular) distance between two objects: then they are distinguishable as *two* objects under best lighting conditions. At any smaller distance only *one,* but brighter or larger, object is seen.

Therefore it is obvious to cover the "celestial sphere" (more precisely, its surface observed from the sphere's center in the interior) with a *grid* whose *mesh size* is about one arc minute. The narrowest grid consists of equilateral triangles (see sketch).

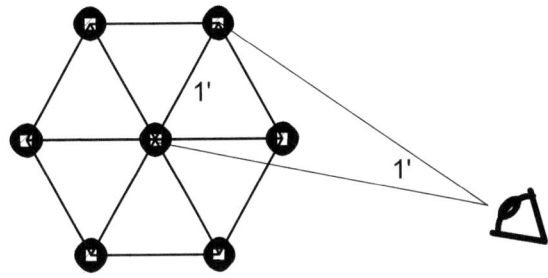

A star is attached to each grid point. It follows that two neighbouring stars always have minimum distance. Each star belongs to 6 triangles, and each triangle has 3 stars at its corners. Alternatively, one can shift the stars to the triangle centers: then every second triangle remains empty, indicating that exactly ½ star has to be counted per triangle.

This model reduces the problem to the question of how many triangles fit into the spherical surface. The number is estimated by dividing the total surface of the sphere by the area of one triangle with about one arc minute "side length". All "lengths" are specified in radians.

Let x denote the side length of the triangle in radians. Then the conversion formula applies

$$\frac{x}{2\pi} = \frac{0,0172°}{360°} \qquad \text{or} \qquad x = 3,002 \times 10^{-4}$$

The area of the triangle surface (base side × height × ½) is

$$A_\Delta = \tfrac{1}{2} x \left(\tfrac{x}{2} \sqrt{3} \right)$$

Hence n triangles fit into the surface of the sphere (4π in radians), i.e.

$$n \left(\tfrac{1}{4} x^2 \sqrt{3} \right) = 4\pi \qquad \text{or} \qquad n = \frac{16\pi}{\sqrt{3}\, x^2}$$

The maximum number N of stars distinguishable to the naked eye on the entire surface of the sphere (with ½ star per triangle) is half the number of triangles

$$N = \frac{8\pi}{\sqrt{3}\, x^2} = 1,6102 \times 10^8 \simeq 161 \text{ millions}$$

Hence from a given point on Earth, about 80 million stars are recognizable (in the meaning of distinguishable) in the sky's *hemisphere*.

This leads to the final question: What does this figure mean for the number of people on this planet?

Afterword

The year 2024 marks the 75th anniversary of the publication date of the dystopian novel "1984" by George Orwell (pseudonymous of Eric Blair).

In this novel, *dictatorship* is defined in a mathematically precise way: namely by its properties. There are essentially three core properties:

- Total narrative synchronisation: *Big Brother* is always right. Everything else is a lie and/or disinformation.

- Permanent distortion of history up to historical fakes.

- Excessive use of pompous words from the "relic box" for brainwashing the people. You know them all already - I'll save myself from the trouble of listing them in detail.

Other specialities include

- *doublethink*, especially double moral standards,

- the hate campaigns,

- *newspeak* and its principles.

My US paperback edition from Signet Classics (reprint 1964) contains an afterword by Erich Fromm (© 1961), which in my opinion is still highly relevant in 2024 and deals with the literary (positive and negative utopias) and political context of the work: for example, *doublethink* was already in use at that time (1961).

I have serious doubts as to whether humanity is currently using the granted period of shrinkage until 2060 to solve its internal problems. At first glance, it looks more as if "1984" is currently being understood primarily as a *guide to action* rather than as a *warning* – but perhaps I am subject to a distortion of perception.

Final question. What is your estimate for the life expectancy of a civilisation, which has made itself 100% dependent on microelectronics and digitalisation?
A hint: *Miyake* events (see Part 3, Link 3).

The consequences and collateral damages of unresolved internal problems are of course still in the race and can drastically shorten the timeframe.

The future is open.

Baraka bashad
Paul Nucleus